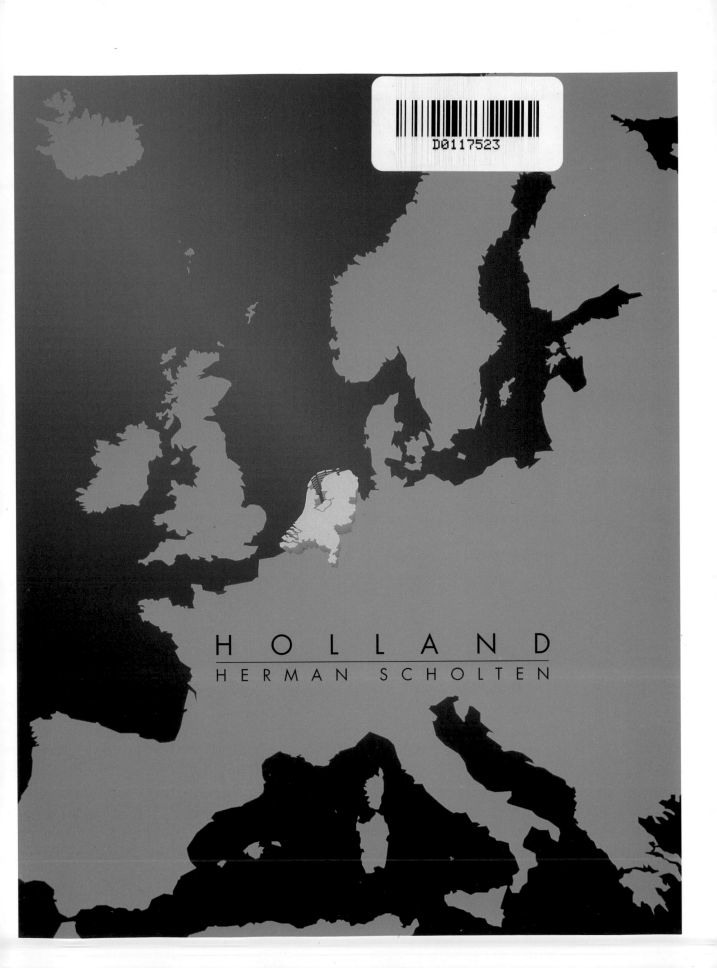

HOLLAND
HERMAN SCHOLTEN

Copyright:
Uitgeverij Van Mastrigt en Verhoeven
P. O. Box 176
6920 AD Duiven
The Netherlands

Compilation and photography:
Herman Scholten

Responsibility for other photographs:
World View Fototheek: pages 1, 5, 43 (2x), 65 (2x), 69 (1x), 80 (2x)
Capital Press Schiphol/Amsterdam: pages 6 (2x), 28 and 29 (2x), 120 (1x), 121 (1x), 123 (1x)
KLM Aerocarto: pages 24, 25, 57
Bloemenveiling Aalsmeer: pages 28 and 29 (5x)
Frits Gerritsen, Marken: page 38 (1x top)
Henk van der Leeden, Marken: pages 38 (1x bottom), 39 (1x)
Robas B.V. Weesp: pages 58 and 59
Wim Janszen, Harderwijk: pages 60 (1x), 63 (5x)
Aerophoto Schiphol: pages 71 (1x), 72 (1x), 91, 96
Rijksmuseum Paleis Het Loo, E. Boeijinga: pages 88, 89
Ministerie van Verkeer en Waterstaat: page 105 (1x)
Aeroview Zestienhoven: pages 111 (1x) 113 (4x)

Text:
D. van Koten, Rotterdam

Printing:
Tamminga Siegers
Nieuwgraaf 300
6921 RS Duiven

Lithography:
Nederlof Repro
Spaarneweg 12
2142 EN Heemstede

Publication and Distribution:
Uitgeverij Van Mastrigt en Verhoeven
P.O. Box 176
6920 AD Duiven

Translation:
CopyTrust, Rotterdam

ISBN: 90-73296-15-3

Holland, one big party!

That's the way a foreign friend described several days spent touring the towns and countryside of the Netherlands. It was more a case of politeness than enthusiasm that had persuaded him to take the journey to the Low Countries in what is for him the far north. The journey began at Schiphol, Amsterdam.

During the landing, in beautiful weather, the aircraft circled low over Amsterdam. The friend was at once amazed by the radial network of canals that seem to encircle the city with rings of self-confidence. The idea that Schiphol was a polder under sea-level did not mean very much to him.

Amsterdam was so surprisingly nearby, just like everything in the rest of the journey. The scale of houses and towns in Holland is small. Merchants' mansions have no surrounding grounds because they are built economically in rows. Even the Dutch population seems to be like that. They squeeze in, make way and definitely do not stand out. Sometimes the Dutch need a foreign friend to point this out to them!

God created the world, but the Dutch made Holland.

The Haarlemmermeer where Schiphol Airport lies, does not explain this very clearly. But directly north of Amsterdam, the name Waterland is an excellent example. Tiny pieces of land seem to float in a limitless number of pools. Leeghwater had the North Holland lakes drained in the seventeenth century. Along the banks of the Zuider Zee we come across numerous small towns which look like Amsterdam but are smaller and have less high buildings. From the air we see an impressive picture of the land north of the Afsluitdijk. Holland's far north that is not called Holland, but Groningen and Friesland. The Wadden Sea, the cradle of many rare species of European birds is a unique tidal area which stretches into Denmark. Separating the Wadden Sea and the North Sea are the Wadden Islands. The environmentalists are busy here, and no new drilling rig goes unnoticed. The risks caused by exploitation are high, because the largest gas deposit of Europe lies under this sea and land.

The agricultural land in Groningen and Friesland strongly resembles Holland. Water sports are an important activity in Friesland, and in Groningen there are extensive farmlands that would not look out of place, as regards size, in the Middle West of the U.S.A. The old fortifications on the borders of Groningen and Drenthe remind us that freedom did not come easily, but had to be fought for.

In Drenthe we are in the 'higher' Low Countries which includes the whole of the east and south, right into Noord-Brabant.

The Hunebedden in Drenthe, prehistoric graves from the early Stone Age and built of heavy stone blocks from the last Ice Age, are one of the oldest signs of human existence in the Netherlands. The top of Overijssel is like the wet, flat Holland that we could see on the other side of the Zuider Zee. The towns are even smaller and water sport more important still.

The River IJssel winds towards the IJsselmeer and down stream are the old Hanseatic towns that were already important when the towns of Holland had hardly begun their history. It was ideal countryside for knights to build their strategic forts. Then their noble offspring richly decorated the woodlands of the Achterhoek and Twente with country mansions. The Oranges built Het Loo, their country seat on the Veluwe for leisure pursuits and hunting. Where the Rhine splits into the Waal, Rhine and IJssel is the gateway to Holland through which foreign armies invaded, until they came to a halt in Utrecht where the sandy soil gives way to wetter areas. Such a transition takes place in the city of Utrecht, the Roman Ultrajectum. It is now the central point in the road and railway networks of the Netherlands.

The River Vecht winds from here to the north, and where it reaches the Zuider Zee at Muiden was a natural location for Muider Castle, a medieval fort built for the protection of Amsterdam.

The big rivers form a border with the southern Netherlands.

The Maas comes from the south. Maastricht is the first and oldest city of the Netherlands with an unmistakable Limburg accent. The River Maas has formed a borderline with Belgium since 1830. North of Venlo, the German border is within range of a cannon ball, at least it was in 1815. Den Bosch, the capital of Noord-Brabant, was once the fourth city of Brabant, a province that stretched into Belgium way beyond Brussels.

Eindhoven, the Philips town, is now the largest city of the south. Vlissingen which lies in the mouth of the Schelde is the key to the port of Antwerp. The Dutch and Zeelanders knew about this some centuries ago, and the Allies came to the same conclusion at the end of the Second World War. But despite the violence of the last war and also in the Eighty Years' War, nature was always the greatest threat. The methods used to restrain the sea in the delta of Rhine, Maas and Schelde have become more complicated over the centuries. The Delta Works, the closure of the open estuaries in Zeeland and Zuid-Holland, evoked admiration everywhere.

The entrances to the ports of Antwerp and Rotterdam remained open. And Rotterdam has been proud for many years to call itself the largest port in the world. The gigantic port and industries of the Rotterdam area show us a different face of Holland. On the edge of this area is Kinderdijk, nineteen windmills in a row which visitors from all over the world come to see. And here too are numerous old towns which foreigners, including our friend, will find fascinating.

The country behind the dunes, where clay and sand mingle, provides ideal soil for growing flower bulbs. A phenomenon that actually dates back to the seventeenth century when Holland discovered the world and new products from all the corners of the earth were brought here.

I wanted to tell my friend that we had learnt about bulbs from his homeland, but the proximity of Schiphol made conversation impossible for a while.

No matter, he was already enthusiastic about Holland!

4 INDEX

Ground Control

At the bottom of the former Haarlemmermeer (lake), some four metres under sea-level is one of the most modern and busy airports in the world, Luchthaven Schiphol (Amsterdam Airport). Where once ships used to disappear under the waves, a giant of the air now lifts off or lands on Mother Earth every five minutes.

Control Tower

Panorama

Runway

This junction of international air traffic covers some 1700 hectares of land. It is the home base of KLM the oldest airline company in the world that has been operating for three-quarters of a century.

The train and road connections are ideal. The A4 motorway (Amsterdam-The Hague) runs alongside the airport, and the railway even runs underneath.

Noord-Zuid Hollands Koffiehuis

(Top) Central Station

Schreiers Tower

Central Station was built in the last century as a barrier between the old docks on the River IJ and the city. The docks have been relocated to the west and the railway station is now the ideal entrance for a visit to the city centre. All the trams and city buses depart from here. Canal cruise boats are moored nearby and the Metro station is located under the Koffiehuis. From Central Station, the Damrak leads us on to the Dam square, the heart of the city. There are more canal cruise boats waiting here, and we see the famous Beurs built by the

Damrak

Beurs

architect Berlage in 1903. In those days people were used to an abundance of neo-classical styles and this new building caused quite a stir. Now it is a monument itself in a monumental city. St Nicholas Church opposite the Koffiehuis is not much older.

St Nicholaas Church

Palace on the Dam

A dam was built in the River Amstel more than 700 years ago. Today the Dam is a square in the heart of Amsterdam and also of Holland, and some people even think, of the world. The Royal Palace was originally built as the City Hall in the seventeenth century, the Golden Age of Holland. On the 20th January 1648, a year that brought peace to the Netherlands, the first of 13,659 wooden piles were pounded into the ground. This started the building of Jacob van Campen's design. The master builder and painter designed a building that would reflect the wealth and power of the most influential merchant city of the world. High above the Dam, the Maid of Peace brandishes Mercury's staff and olive leaf, the symbols of trade and peace. Beneath her sits the Maid of the City with the city's arms on her left knee, this is the central figure of the tympanum carved by the Flemish sculptor, Artus Quellinus. The Maid is surrounded by numerous symbolic figures of people and animals; Neptune is among them pointing his awful trident at the Maid.

The Palace is crowned by a copper dome which houses the carillon that weighs a massive 38,000 kilogrammes, and was made by the Hemony brothers. Neither money nor trouble was spared when building the City Hall. During French rule the City Hall became a Royal Palace, and it remains so to this day. Next to Palace, a little hidden and pushed to one side is the Nieuwe Kerk (New Church) where the inauguration of Queen Beatrix took place. Building began in 1490, but the church and its monumental tower could not be finished, because after the completion of the City Hall in 1655 there was no money available. A city-council always has to set priorities. On the other side of the square is the National Monument. Here on the 4th May each year, those who died in the war are remembered in silence and flowers are laid in tribute.

National Monument

Feeding the pigeons   *Prinsengracht/Brouwersgracht* ▼

On other days there are many other kinds of visitors. The pigeons are always there. The Nieuwezijds Voorburgwal with the former Post Office behind the Palace is often thought by unsuspecting tourists to be the real Palace. Behind here the "grachtengordel" (canal network) begins with the Singel.

Magna Plaza

Wester Church

The Singel lies outside the old city centre. The first canal which the merchants built outside the centre was appropriately named: Herengracht (Gentlemen's Canal). Later on there was time for the emperor's canal and then the prince's: Keizersgracht and Prinsengracht. The order of importance is obvious.
On the Prinsengracht is the Wester Church topped with its golden coloured emperor's crown, a church made famous in song. Rembrandt is buried there and a little further along there is the Anne Frank House where Anne wrote her diary.

The city grew prosperously like a tree, adding a new ring each year. The canal houses can be distinguished by their ornamental gables, from left to right: cornice, step, neck, spout and bell gables.

Anne Frank House

Left to right: cornice, step, neck, spout and bell gables

Leidsegracht

A densely populated city built on water needs a large number of bridges. There are about 1200 in Amsterdam, and a third of these are in the so-called "grachtengordel" (canal network). The famous Magere Bridge (Skinny Bridge) spans the Amstel. This is an eye-catcher, especially when illuminated at night. Less striking, but interesting to those with an eye for detail, are gable stones that can tell us much about the history of the canal buildings and their occupants.

Magere Bridge

Oudezijdskolk   *Korte Prinsengracht*   *Oudezijdskolk*   *Brouwersgracht*   *Oudezijdskolk*

Munt Tower

Zuider Church   Montelbaans Tower ▶

When the city expanded, after 1585, the Munt Tower and the Montelbaans Tower lost their function. In 1606, the Montelbaans Tower acquired a baroque tower crown from Hendrick de Keyser. He was also the architect who designed and built the Zuider Church of 1614, one of the oldest and largest protestant churches in the Netherlands.

Panorama of River Amstel and the Stopera

Panorama of Amstel with Magere Bridge

Back again on the Amstel near the Magere Bridge (Skinny Bridge). The bridge is named after the Mager sisters who had property on the other side of the Amstel and the city council provided them access by building a bridge in 1671. A little way along is Theater Carré. This was built in the last century as a circus ring and it is now the mecca of Dutch entertainers.
The new Stopera (City Hall and Opera of Amsterdam) is situated along the Amstel in the heart of the old city.

Theater Carré

7, Singel

There are not only grand and luxurious canal buildings; house no. 7 on the Singel is said to be the narrowest and smallest house in Amsterdam. It is a favourite topic for the information given on the many tourist canal boats that cruise here on their way through the Haarlemmer Lock towards Central Station or the open water of the River IJ.

Little Amsterdammers

The Round or New Lutheran Church on the Singel was completed in 1671 and is now used as a hall for exhibitions and conferences of the nearby Sonesta Hotel. Amsterdam has not been built for cars.

Parking is one of its main problems. Attempts by the city council to limit inconvenience to pedestrians has resulted in the well-known anti-parking posts marked with the three St Andrew's crosses of the city arms. The posts soon became known as "little Amsterdammers" and are often painted in pretty colours. They are now used in other towns, but without the crosses and not painted so nicely.

18 AMSTERDAM

On the Singel, close to the Munt Tower is the Flower Market of Amsterdam. From here you can walk through the Leidsestraat (only open to trams and pedestrians) on to the Leidseplein. This square with its pavement cafes, bars, Stadsschouwburg (City Theatre) and the nearby Holland Casino, is the centre of the city's nightlife. When Ajax wins the football cup, this is the place where the fans assemble, in front of the balcony of the Stadsschouwburg.

Flower Market

Holland Casino

Leidseplein

Museumplein is a more suitable square for larger crowds. It lies behind the stately building of the Rijksmuseum (1885) built by the architect Cuypers. Amsterdam Central Station is another example of his work.

Stadsschouwburg

Rijksmuseum

In the Rijksmuseum, we can see many famous paintings from the Dutch Golden Age; Rembrandt's 'The Night Watch' is the public's favourite. The Stedelijk Museum and Van Gogh Museum are also situated on this square. The latter museum which is the newest, continues to attract an increasing number of visitors.

The Night Watch

Vincent van Gogh

Stopera

Waterlooplein

The building of the new Amsterdam City Hall was not without its critics. The merging of the project with the building of an opera produced a combination of City Hall and opera house, the Stopera. Two problems could be solved in one go, and Amsterdam has already become used to the effect.

During construction, the famous flea market on Waterlooplein was moved temporarily.

's Lands Zeemagazijn was a warehouse built in 1656 for the Admiralty to a design of Daniel Stalpaert. It is now a suitable home for the Nederlands Scheepvaartmuseum (Dutch Maritime Museum). The days of the Verenigde Oostindisch Compagnie (Dutch East India Company) come alive in a fabulous collection. A remarkable replica of a merchant ship of the Golden Age is an immediate eye-catcher.

Maritime Museum

(Top) Prinseneiland

Prinsengracht

In the Golden Age, a number of beautiful warehouses and commercial buildings were built on the east side of the old city at Brouwersgracht and on the west side, on Prinseneiland. Many of these buildings have fortunately not been demolished, but particularly in recent decades, renovated and refurbished for residential purposes. It is now a privilege to live there.

Brouwersgracht

Amsterdam citizens do not only love to live at the water's edge, but also on the water. The numerous houseboats turned the disadvantage of the post-war housing shortage into an advantage.

River Amstel

Prins Hendrikkade

In the end, the city council had to take steps to curb the growth. Even though housing is no longer in such short supply, a houseboat remains an ideal solution for many people.

Nieuwe Keizersgracht

Herengracht

There are now houseboats of every shape and size in all the canals of the city. The daily life of Amsterdam is reflected, literally and figuratively, in the water of the canals.
The six hundred canals have a total length of more than one hundred kilometres.

Herengracht

Oudezijds Voorburgwal

This fine network of waterways was built by spades, wheelbarrows and a huge amount of sweat, and it is a drainage system that still serves the city daily.

Brouwersgracht

This is without doubt the most famous view of Amsterdam from the air, the network of canals that radiate like rings of self confidence across the city. When the network was built, the cartographer Bleau lived and worked in this city. The bird's eye view was then a figment of the imagination and the view from church towers. From the centre right of the picture, the River Amstel runs past the Stopera, fanning out in different directions. Above centre is the nineteenth century Central Station where the Amstel used to flow into the River IJ before the Dam was built, and long before the building of the railway station formed a barrier between the old city and the IJ. At the end of the last century, the Rokin, south of the Dam was filled in. Bottom right, the Stadsschouwburg is visible on Leidseplein. And throughout the entire picture working from the inside to the outer edge is firstly the Singel, then the Herengracht, Keizersgracht and Prinsengracht. When naming the Herengracht (the Gentlemen's Canal) the powerful citizens of the Golden Age were honouring themselves.

Keizersgracht was named in memory of Emperor Maximilian I, the holy Roman ruler from Austria who gave the city a symbolic crown in 1489 because Amsterdam did not have a coat of arms. The Prinsengracht was named in honour of Prince William of Orange.

Holland Casino

It has become a tradition over the years to cheerfully illuminate the city centre. Not only Leidseplein and other night-spots but also Rembrandtplein and Thorbeckeplein. And not just party lights at the waterside, but the old canal houses are specially illuminated, and the arches of the bridges participate in the festivities. Modern buildings too, like the Stopera, play their part in the fanfare of light.

Keizersgracht 123

Leidsegracht/Herengracht

Flower Market

Panorama of River Amstel

Even sales at the Flower Market continue under the fairy lights.

Yet Amsterdam by night is not a quiet fairy tale town but a bustling city where visitors feel at home. Sometimes audaciously lit, sometimes modestly, but always surprising and fascinating. Even for Amsterdammers who are used to the sights.

This is again the famous Magere Bridge over the Amstel, but now illuminated. The neo-classical Rijksmuseum is bathed in a sea of light.

The lights are traditional to Amsterdam. In the last year of the war, the starving Amsterdammers used to sing "when the lights go on again on Leidseplein." Because only then would the war be over.

Herengracht

Rijksmuseum

Flower Auction

"When it's spring again, I'll bring again, tulips from Amsterdam...". At least that's how the song goes. But tulips from Amsterdam originate in the bulb growing area, and cut-flowers and plants come from the auction hall at Aalsmeer. Flowers have been cultivated in the Aalsmeer area since 1850, at first in the open fields and recently in greenhouses.
The huge range of flowers and presence of the largest flower auction in the world ensures a leading position which they are rightly proud of.

Auction ▶

Geranium Greenhouse

Auction Hall

Aalsmeer demonstrates this prominence in organising the famous annual flower parade when a long procession of floats with thousands of flowers forms a festive and magnificent show.
Besides this event, the National Flower Trade Exhibition is held annually in Aalsmeer. Growers and merchants from all over the world come to learn about new varieties and new horticultural technology.

There are other flower and plant auctions in the Netherlands, and even areas where cultivation is more important than here, but the Aalsmeer auction remains unique.

The proximity of Amsterdam Airport is a great advantage to the Aalsmeer auction. Flowers are certainly a fleeting product and the time between auction and selling to consumers has to be as short as possible.

Export by air

This was why the flower growing areas were originally concentrated in the densely populated regions in the west of the Netherlands.

And, because of the proximity of Amsterdam Airport, a bouquet of flowers from Holland can soon be for sale on Broadway, New York.

Flowers from Holland are a common sight in many other places throughout the world.

Town Hall

Gravestenen Bridge

Panorama of River Spaarne

An unsuspecting visitor standing in front of the Town Hall on the Grote Markt might receive a flower from a local beauty who is better known as the Haarlem Flower Girl. This civic promotion underlines the fact that this town and its environs have been an important centre for the cultivation and trade in flower bulbs for centuries.

The Grote Markt (Market Square) is dominated by the medieval, old and grey St Bavo Church, the most venerable building among the thousands of monuments in this town on the River Spaarne.

St Bavo

Frans Hals Museum

Teylers hofje

Hofje van Noblet

Amsterdamse Poort

Haarlem is also the town of the renowned artist Frans Hals and there is a museum of that name in the Oudemannenhuis building which dates from 1606.

This town is abundant with interesting details. fascinating towers, quiet courtyards (hofjes), crammed antique shops, varying views of the river, signboards and wall plaques, in fact too much to mention. The Amsterdamse Poort is a well conserved medieval gateway.

Kalverringdijk

The Zaanse Schans recalls memories of a glorious past. In an hexagonal bulwark where once the Sea Beggars resisted a seige of the Spanish army, a picturesque Zaan neighbourhood has been reconstructed with excellent examples of traditional Zaan timbered buildings.

It caused quite a stir before work could begin on the open-air museum, the brainchild of architect Jacob Schepper.

't Koopmanshuys

Paltrok Windmill "De Gekroonde Poelenburg" 1868

Now a large number of wooden houses that might otherwise have been lost have been brought here. The museum shop is accommodated in a carefully reconstructed Albert Heyn grocery dating from 1887.

Five windmills decorate the banks of the River Zaan. They recall a time when Zaan industry relied on wind power. The Gekroonde Poelenburg mill, top right, is the youngest, and

Mill "Het Prinsenhof" 1722

Paint mill "De Kat" 1782

Oil mill "De Zoeker" 1676

Panorama of Kalverringdijk

has been sawing thick planks of timber since 1868. The oldest windmill, De Zoeker, began to grind oilseed in 1676. The Huisman has been making famous Zaan mustard since 1781. In the middle picture is De Kat (1782), a paint mill.

Panorama of the Zaan

Panorama

In the eighteenth century, Broek in Waterland was the richest village of North Holland.
In the photograph, hidden behind the trees, is the double aisled late gothic Dutch Reformed Church.
The church has timbered arches and contains the grave of the legendary Neeltje Pater, the wealthy wife of a shipowner of the eighteenth century.
Even today, the wealth of Broek in Waterland's residents is above the national average.
It is a unique village, a wonderful place to live with many lovely old houses and timbered gables, a great place to stay whether it be summer or winter. A quiet village not far from Amsterdam.

Seasonal views of centre

Pampus Island

Pampus on the outer reaches of the river,
Buiten-IJ, served as a fort for the city of
Amsterdam for many centuries.
When the ships of the Golden Age sailed into
Amsterdam, Pampus was a formidable obstacle.

· *Panorama of Durgerdam*

Westwal Smack Race

When the ships arrived at Pampus, it meant
days of waiting until the tide and wind would
allow them to pass through the shallow waters
into the IJ.

Durgerdam officially belongs to the city of
Amsterdam. This outpost will, however, never
be urbanised and the park landscape will be

protected. However, there are worries about
Amsterdam's plans to build houses in
Buiten-IJ. Durgerdammers do not like this
idea, and they call it 'horizon pollution'.
But come what may, the almost three hundred
year old white chapel with its sturdy tower
will continue to serve as a beacon for pleasure
craft.

Bell Tower

The Waag, a weigh house on the Middendam and the Bell Tower in the bend of the Noordeinde are on one of the most charming locations of Monnickendam. The Waag was built about 1600 on a corner of the harbour. Sixty years later there was enough money to decorate it with lovely pilaster gables. When the building of the Waag began, the slender Bell Tower had been a captivating sight on the skyline for one hundred years, especially when viewed from the Gouwzee.

Harbour

Ice sailing on the Gouwzee

The construction date and original purpose of the Bell Tower is unknown. The earliest records about the tower were made in 1591. In that year, the brick-built building was given a timbered superstructure which closely resembles the crowned tower of the Old Church in Amsterdam.
The bells were also hung in place in 1591. The first was cast in 1513 and the second in 1591.

Three years later, the town celebrated the arrival of the first series of chiming bells which Pieter van den Ghein cast in Mechelen. In 1597 all the bells on order had been delivered. It is now the only complete carillon of that period in the Netherlands.
One of the oldest trades in Monnickendam, ship-building and repairs, is plied on both sides of the harbour.

Town Hall "de Rijp"

Town Hall "Graft"

The Best Village in Holland. This title of honour (note the capital letters) was given to Rijp by its most eminent son, Jan Adriaensz, also called Leeghwater. The man famous for reclaiming land enriched his village in 1630 by the design of this Town Hall. There are similar town halls in nearby Graft (1613), Groot-Schermer (1639-1652) and Jisp (1650).

Town Hall "Schermer"　　　*Town Hall "Jisp"*

Celebrating the Queen's Birthday, 30 April

Moeniswerf

Kerkbuurt

Traditional costume

When the Zuider Zee was closed in 1932, the Markers discontinued their fishing industry. Once there were 200 fishing boats, and the catch was usually sent to Amsterdam.

In earlier times, the Markers had also been important to Amsterdam, because when the East India ships were moored off the Pampus, a floating ship's lift could help them into the IJ. In those days, the Markers were also engaged in whaling which is probably why Marken wood carving and clothing show Scandinavian influences.

Panorama of the island

Kerkbuurt

Marken was not connected to the mainland until 1957.

When the new causeway was opened numerous tourists could cross by coach. The early fear that the island would lose its identity because of massive tourism, fortunately did not turn out to be true.

The fact that Marken is still surrounded on all sides by water has certainly been important. The water around Marken will remain for the time being. The plans for Markerwaard, the final polder in the former Zuider Zee, have been postponed.

And if the polder does come it will probably be diverted around the former island. The Markers will not be sorry, because an important part of the charm and tourist interest comes from the surrounding water.

Traditional Costume

Is Volendam more of a tourist town than Marken?

The outward signs are the same, but the long physical isolation of Marken as an island could be a reason for this; Volendam was not so isolated. One difference is also the protestantism of Marken and catholicism of Volendam, but this has little effect on the tourist trade. Volendammers have a professional football team and a great many pop groups. Yes, even their own sound, "Eel Beat". There is no place where the eels are fatter, nor the number of pop

Panorama of the harbour

groups greater per square metre than in Volendam.
And look at the lace curtains in the windows.
Folk are always trying to do better than the
neighbours, no money or trouble is spared in
pomp and extravagance. You can't see this
from the air, but it's true!

Harbour in winter

They are tough folk who live here, not afraid to work hard to earn a living.
People who love rugged pastimes like skating on natural ice. In freezing weather, the harbour is turned into a skating rink and when conditions are right, the Volendam skaters take a trip over the Gouwzee to Marken.

Swaying backwards and forwards over the Volendam harbour, could a skater dream of better surroundings? Few tourists have seen Holland's most famous fishing village from this angle.

Doolhof Bridge

In the summer they flock in their thousands through the narrow streets and along the harbour. And what do they see? Here and there an elderly person in traditional costume, a waitress with a pointed hat, some timbered facades and, if they are lucky, a fishing boat. But the tourists keep coming from all corners of the world.

And when one thinks that Volendam was an almost forgotten fishing village on the Zuider Zee for many centuries, where they kept to their own traditions and costume in a self-imposed isolation.

The traditional costumes are now mainly used for the tourists who want to have their photographs taken.

Volendam only developed into a tourist centre after the Afsluitdijk (IJsselmeer Dam) was closed in 1932 when the Zuider Zee became the IJsselmeer.

44 EDAM

Kwakel Bridge

Edam has such charm thanks to the slender Speeltoren (carillon tower) and the classic drawbridges. One of the most lovely bridges is the Kwakel.
The partially timbered houses on the Kwakelsteeg and the leaning carillon tower in the distance are the pride of Edam.

Kapiteinshuis

The tower nearly collapsed in 1972, but they could fortunately divert the danger in time.
On the left is a view of the Scheepmakersdijk with tea pavilions that would not look amiss on the river Vecht which flows through Utrecht.

Schepenmakersdijk

Cheese Market

The history of Edam began in the twelfth century when farmers and fishermen began to settle on the banks of the little river, the IJe. Shipbuilding and trade brought increasing prosperity well into the seventeenth century. Edam is now mainly known as the name of a type of cheese. Edam cheese has been exported all over the world for centuries.

When visiting the Kaaswaag (cheese weigh house) one learns that an Edam always weighs about 1,000 or 1,600 grammes.

The cheese market is held every Wednesday morning in the summer months.

Proveniershuis

Cheese Market

Cheese Market from the air

Cheese Weigh House

Zijdam and Kuipers Bridge

Wildemanshofje

"They weigh up their money and their God carefully." A. Roland Holst wrote this about the Dutch. He might not have meant it too literally, because he lived in Bergen not far from Alkmaar.

He will have seen how they weigh cheese in the Waag on Friday mornings. In fact this building was once a house of God before it was put to commercial use. The cheese carriers move about with shuffling steps.

Broeker Auction

The countryside around Broek op Langedijk has quite rightly been called the 'Kingdom of a Thousand Islands', although nobody has counted all those small pieces of land. Numerous kinds of cabbage and other market garden products used to be sent by barge to the auction house.

Transport by water has given Broek op Langedijk an auction which can be called unique for two reasons.

Boats laden with vegetables are navigated past the auction clock, and the Langedijkers also claim the right to talk about the only 'navigated auction in the world'. They conveniently forget the auction held in Bangkok at the water market, because it is so very far away.

Cabbage field

Schermerpolder

A more truthful claim is the honorary title
"oldest vegetable auction in Europe".
For the first time in July 1887, a barge full of
cabbage was auctioned at the landing stage
near Bakkers bridge.
Later on, a distinctive white building was
erected over the water. This building is now a
museum. At regular times (in the summer)
vegetables are still floated in by barge, and the
auction clock is put to use. But these events are
only to uphold the tradition,

Schermerhorn

50 HOORN

Oosterpoort

Westfries Museum

Opposite one of Hoorn's most beautiful
facades, at the beginning of Houten Hoofd, and
flanked by masts and rigging, the remarkable
semi-round Hoofd Tower (see picture) has been
standing on guard since 1532. Even the
Oosterpoort (see top of page) has survived.
We can learn all about West Friesland's history
in the Westfries museum.
Originally this building (1632) was the seat of
the States Council.

Hoofd Tower

Hoofd Tower

Oosterpoort

Boys of Bontekoe

Weigh House and statue of J.P. Coen

Step and neck gables decorate the old Dutch scenery. Willem Bontekoe, the famous mariner who navigated China and the East Indies lived on the Veermanskade. He made a detailed report of his voyage to the Indies in 1618-1625. Later on Fabricius wrote an adventure book about this voyage "The Ship's Boys of Bontekoe". The ship's boys Padde, Hajo and Rolf are immortalized on the quayside.

Jan Pietersz. Coen stands calmly like a public servant on the Rode Steen, where shortly after the year 1300 the first houses of Hoorn were built. This famous son of Hoorn travelled to the Far East for the Oost-Indische Compagnie (Dutch East India Company) and in 1619 established the new town of Batavia on the ruins of the ravaged Jacatra.

That town is now better known as Djakarta, but at the time Coen really wanted to call it Nieuw-Hoorn.

Spui

The houses on the Spui (top photo) have not been leaning together for long. Shortly after the war, they were completely reconstructed from old drawings. The differences in roof height, lack of straight lines and the tangle of extensions is all clever restoration work. The houses are a testimony of the respect Enkhuizers have for the past, and it also demonstrates their resilience.

Zuider Zee Museum and Compagnie bridge

This old warehouse of the Verenigde Oost-Indische Compagnie is now the home of the interesting and richly furnished Binnenmuseum (indoor museum) of the Zuider Zee Museum. An excellent starting point for a visit to the museum and a stroll past the many lovely buildings and dreamy canals which are witness to the wealth of the past.

Through view

Koepoort

A moat and bastions still guard Enkhuizen. Fishermen continue to unload their abundant catches at the foot of the Dromedaris. For many years, the Enkhuizers lived in a dying town on the Zuider Zee, but some years after the completion of the Afsluitdijk (IJsselmeer Dam) they managed to raise their heads above water again. Other fishing communities on the Zuider Zee gave up the struggle after the Afsluitdijk (IJsselmeer Dam) closed in 1932, casting aside their boats. But the Enkhuizers never gave up. The rich fishing of the IJsselmeer now provides a good living. The other ports are only stopovers or moorings for pleasure craft and sailing boats.

The Dromedaris was completed in 1540 as part of the fortifications. Twenty-five years later, the Hemony brothers received an order to cast carillon of 24 bells for the little dome tower. music still rings out over the harbours ding areas.

Harbour

Local villains were once imprisoned in the tower rooms, later on students used them for parties and staying overnight, and now exhibitions are held there.

Dromedaris

Radboud Castle

Town Hall

This building is still called Radboud Castle, but it is only a quarter of the almost square fortress that Floris V had built near Medemblik in the late thirteen century to subdue the West Frisians. Two of the corner towers and a large part of the outside walls were reduced to rubble to reinforce the West Frisian sea dam in 1578.

The Town Hall is considerably younger, built in 1939 in old Dutch style. The honour of being the oldest town in West-Friesland goes to Medemblik, the smallest of the three largest towns. Town privileges were granted in 1289, Enkhuizen followed in 1355 and Hoorn in 1356. Medemblik is now known mainly as a centre for water sport recreation.

Gable of Burgerweeshuis   *Harbour*   *"De Herder" windmill*

The navy is ever present in Den Helder. The Koninklijk Instituut voor de Marine is a training school for navy officers.
The submarine of the Marine Museum is within walking distance of a Russian submarine, which received its last resting place in the centre of Den Helder, after friendly relations had developed with Russia.
Yet Den Helder is more than just a navy town.

Huisduinen Lighthouse

Russian submarine (top)

Marine Museum (centre)

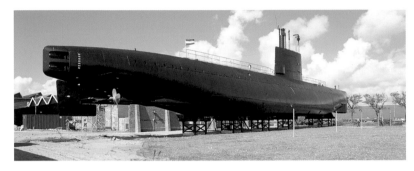

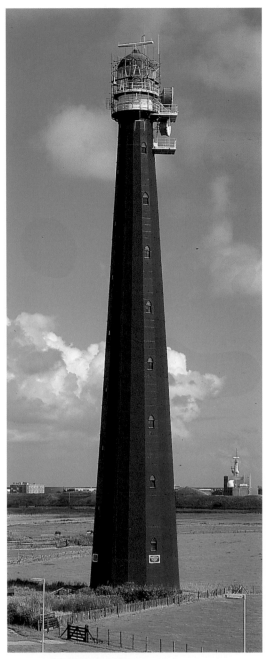

Den Helder-Texel Ferry

The ferry to the island of Texel departs from here, and a short distance from the coast are the busy shipping lanes of the North Sea.
The lighthouse keeps watch over all this activity.

Marine Museum

Panorama from the Monument

Monument

It was on 28 May 1932, and only after the Wieringermeer had been drained that the Afsluitdijk (IJsselmeer Dam) from Noord-Holland to Friesland was closed. A motorway was built on the land originally intended for the railway. But before that happened, in 1954, Cornelis Lely, the great man behind the Zuider Zee project was honoured by a statue.

The continuous flow of water to the IJsselmeer needs to be regularly discharged. There are five discharge sluices built into the dam for this purpose.

Statue of Cornelis Lely

Monument with info-boards

Bird's eye view of the Afsluitdijk

Two on the Frisian side in Kornwerderzand (Lorentz sluices) and three, shown in the photo, on the Noord-Holland side near Den Oever (Stevin sluices). These sluices also have locks for ships up to 2,000 tons. Before the Afsluitdijk was closed, Wieringermeer, the first of the five intended polders was already dry land; the Noord-Oostpolder followed in 1942, and Oostelijk Flevoland in 1956. Zuidelijk Flevoland then became the last polder for the time being, because a ruling about the fifth and final polder, Markerwaard, has been postponed.

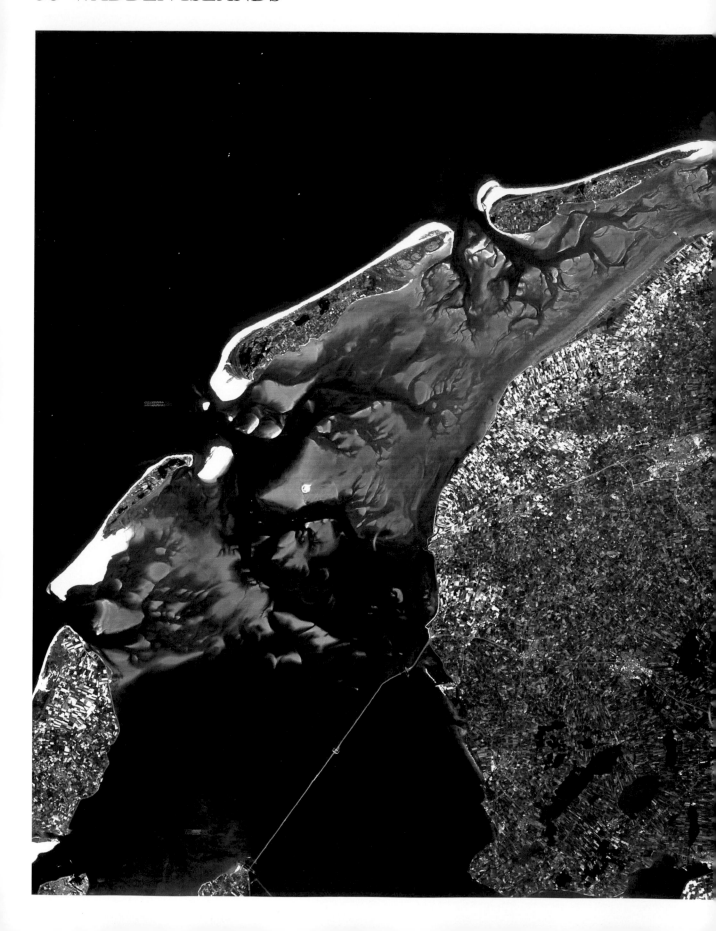

Satellite picture

This is a wonderful satellite picture of the Wadden area. Below left is the island of Texel and the tip of Noord-Holland near Den Helder. The Afsluitdijk draws a straight line from the former Wieringen island to the Frisian coast with a slight kink near the coast at Kornwerderzand.

In the darker Wadden Sea between Kornwerderzand and Texel we can see the lighter spots of sea between land and water. The Wadden is the unique tidal area between the North Sea islands and the coast, stretching from Den Helder across two German borders to Esbjerg in Denmark.

The Dutch Wadden Islands in the photo are from bottom left: Texel, Vlieland, Terschelling, Ameland and Schiermonnikoog. The uninhabited Dutch islands of Rottumerplaat and Rottumeroog are not in the picture. The National Association for the preservation of the Wadden Sea is the largest and most active Dutch environmental association.

The last piece of the Wadden Sea to be turned into polder some decades ago was the Lauwerszee, which shows up clearly in the top right of the picture.

Large-scale impoldering is unacceptable now, but there are other dangers for the Wadden association to guard against. Oil and gas exploitation is just one example of a controversial issue.

60 TEXEL

The Wadden Islands have only been recently inhabited; between AD 800 and 1100. Only Texel is different. Archaeological digs revealed not only traces of prehistoric times but also signs of the early Middle Ages. In about the year 900 Texel was deserted. The village of Den Hoorn and the church with the white tower date from the fifteen century, but the settlement had been established earlier and was relocated at that time.

Lighthouse

(Centre right) De Slufter

Den Hoorn

Harbour, Oude Schild

Sheep fold

Lighthouse

The name of the village, Oost-Vlieland (East Vlieland), indicates that there was also a West-Vlieland. The latter was engulfed by the sea nearly three centuries ago. Alluvion has since caused new land to form, but this flatland, Hors, is uninhabited and used by the air force for exercises and target practice. Oost-Vlieland grew to its greatest prosperity and size in the first half of the seventeenth century. But little remains of this: a number of seventeenth century step gables on the Dorpsstraat, the church, the poor house and the Tromphuys. The latter is probably the oldest building in Vlieland, but it was not until 1896 that the then occupants gave it the name of the great admiral Maarten Harpertsz. Tromp.

Through view

Former Town Hall

Dorpsstraat

Brandaris Lighthouse

The Brandaris lighthouse has stood on this spot since the beginning of the seventeenth century. The previous lighthouse was then destroyed by the sea. There are a few commodore houses in West which survived the fire and devastation caused by the English in 1665.

▼ *"Friesland" Ferryboat*   *"Koegelwieck" Speedboat* ▼

Harbour

Buoy depot

Het Behouden Huys museum is established in two of these commodore houses, the museum's name is derived from the shelter on Novaya Zemlya of Willem Barents (a son of the island of Terschelling).

Het Behouden Huys Museum

Sorgdrager Museum

Ameland has also lost land to the sea, and continues to do so. Erosion on the west side has already cost dearly and yet a permanent coastline can be maintained.
In the middle of the island, north of Nes,

Commodore house

Public bicycle pump

bathing pavilions and hotels were swallowed up by waves a decade ago. But nature gives back the land in the east.
Nevertheless, the struggle with the sea still continues on this nature friendly Wadden island.
Nearly all motorised traffic is banned on Ameland, but fortunately the public facilities for cycling are of a high standard. The holiday makers who are nature and peace lovers profit the most from the ban.

Oystercatchers

Stonechat

Common terns

Shelducks

Lesser black-backed gulls

Waterpoort

The Waterpoort in Sneek has been standing since 1613; and fortunately in 1878 was renovated to its former glory.
The lonely monument curator of the time, Victor de Stuers, prevented not only the threatened demolition, but also restored it to its original state. When, much later, a canal was filled in, they spared a piece of the canal, because otherwise the Waterpoort (Water Gate) would be left standing high and dry.

Sneek Week on Snekermeer

Sneek (the Frisians call it "Snits") is the prominent Frisian water sport town in the heart of the Frisian lakeland. Frisian and non-Frisians alike can heartily enjoy themselves on the lakes, especially during Sneek Week at the beginning of August.

Wip mill on Prinses Margriet Canal

Traditional costume

In order to boost the local economy, at the turn of the century a number of Frisian patrons had youngsters from Hindeloopen learn the old skills of painting. Hindeloopen painting has become a rage, particularly in recent decades. All kinds of objects are now painted in this style which people had never thought about painting before, such as milk churns and clothes hangers. But the real money earner for Hindeloopen is the large yacht harbour which has been in use since 1960.

Lock keeper's house

The Mistress of Stavoren

Harbour

In the nineteenth century, Stavoren was even smaller than it is now, and visitors could see ruins, boarded up houses and gardens full of weeds. Later on there was some development which was initially helped by the Zuider Zee fishing industry (with their own type of ships, the Stavoren yawl) and later on by the introduction of the ferry service from Stavoren to Enkhuizen.

Nowadays it is mainly water sport that is important. Stavoren is the home port for clippers, old barges and other sailing boats used by holiday makers.

Happily, the old waterway to the yacht harbour has been restored, along with the drawbridge.

Drawbridge

Noorderhaven

Harlingen did not originally have an inner harbour, but around 1600 the growth of the town and the prospering trade prompted its construction.
The Noorderhaven was first, and in the seventeenth and eighteenth century was developed with warehouses, housing and inns. Because of the economic recession during the French era, all this remained in tact. Harlingen has a respectable monument list and the Noorderhaven is a living monument, which the magnificent Town Hall greatly complements.

Zuiderhaven

Havenmantsje

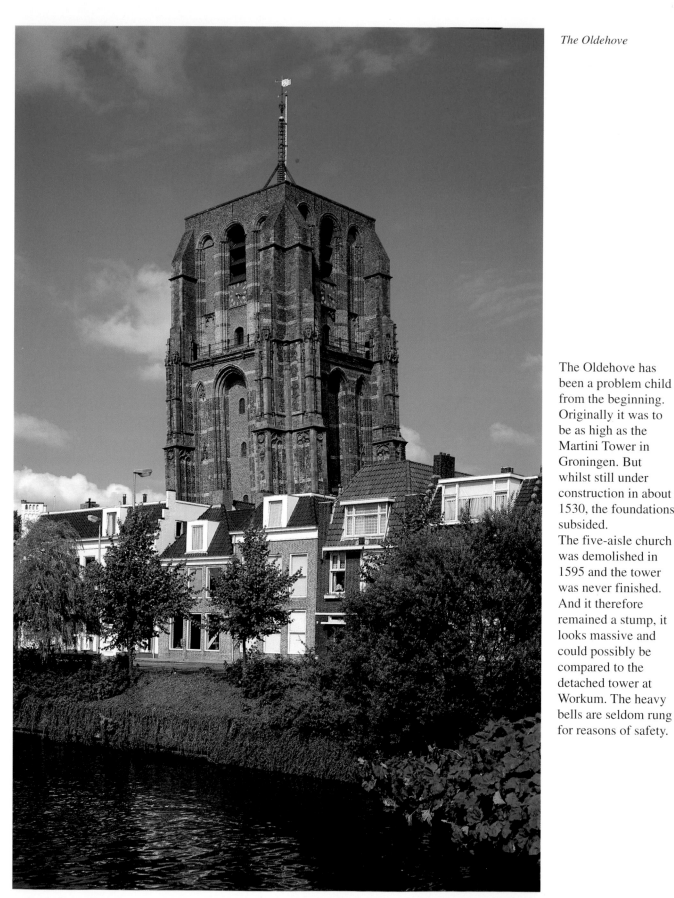

The Oldehove

The Oldehove has been a problem child from the beginning. Originally it was to be as high as the Martini Tower in Groningen. But whilst still under construction in about 1530, the foundations subsided.

The five-aisle church was demolished in 1595 and the tower was never finished. And it therefore remained a stump, it looks massive and could possibly be compared to the detached tower at Workum. The heavy bells are seldom rung for reasons of safety.

Weigh House

City Centre

Leeuwarden cannot boast a row of monumental buildings. But a number are quite striking, because they are all in the city centre. The villages of Oldehove, Nijehove and Hoek were merged in the Middle Ages, and they can all be seen in a walk that takes no more than an hour. At least if one only walks around the outskirts. And in wintry weather, you could see most of them when ice-skating.

Fun on the ice near the Oldehove

The Groninger Museum has acquired a controversial new building on the Verbindingskanaal. A walkway connects it to the railway station on one side and the centre of the city on the other.

(Top) Groninger Museum

This sparkling sundial dating from 1730 is in the Prinsenhof garden on the Turfsingel. The Prinsenhof which dates from 1594 is now the home of Radio Noord.

Prinsenhof

Martini Church

The Martini Tower, 96 metres high, is the second highest tower in the Netherlands. The spire and set of bells were destroyed by a bonfire in 1577. In 1627 reconstruction began on "the old Grey Man". The tower sports a golden horse as a wind vane. The story goes that there was a Roman church situated here in about 1200. Building began on a gothic basilican cruciform church in the middle of the fifteenth century. The church is remarkable for the wide side aisles with five facades which were restored to their original state in the sixties. In 1923, unique and important murals were found in the nave of the chancel, a Christmas cycle of eight depictions and an Easter cycle of six depictions, dating from the early sixteenth century.

Interior of Martini Church

Post mill

In 1607 the Bourtange fortification was reinforced and extended with a crown-work to which sometime later two horn-works were added. After the end of the Eighty Years' War (1648) the bastion suffered from neglect. But in 1665 when the Bishop of Munster was menacing the Westerwolde countryside, the fortification was reinforced. The Bishop was therefore unsuccessful in capturing the bastion in 1672.

In about 1740 the bastion was so run down that it needed more repair and improvement. Work was even done on extensions in 1796, but at the time this kind of fortification was already obsolete. Yet it was not until 1851 that Bourtange ended its function as a military fort, and in 1859 the streets, square and roads were handed over to the local civilian authorities. Bourtange has been repaired and reconstructed as much as possible in recent years. It is a modern tribute to the builders of all those fortifications of the sixteenth and seventeenth centuries.

It is almost a wonder that Bourtange has risen again and become such an impressive sight from the air.

Bourtange from the air

Hunebed Rolde

The lonely shepherd wanders over the peaceful heath. Drenthe still has heath, shepherds and flocks of sheep. And this province is also unique for its Hunebedden, prehistoric sepulchral mounds. A total of 53 prehistoric graves built in the early Stone Age from boulders of the last Ice Age.

"Bartje"

Roderwolde "Woldzigt" 1852

Drenthe has other remarkable features nowadays, for instance the giant radio telescopes of the Westerbork observatory which has been in operation since 1955.
In Assen is a statue of Bartje, the little boy from Anne de Vries' famous novel.
The boy who hated the staple diet of brown beans, and for which he refused to say grace. His feelings represent the pragmatic approach of the Drenthe people.

Westerbork Radio Telescopes

Orvelte is a typical Drenthe village, where little has changed and therefore little has been spoilt. Villages of this kind are rare in our modern times. And the lovers of the art of rural building will be pleased to learn that Orvelte is not only beautifully preserved but that they decided to make it even more beautiful. Unauthentic features were erased, mistakes corrected, existing farmhouses and outhouses restored, and one or two endangered buildings were transported from other places and carefully moulded into the landscape.

Leaving one's car at the parking lot outside the village (there is no space for it in the village) take a stroll through Orvelte and you will get an attractive view of a village in Drenthe.

The city dweller cannot not only see what it was like in a traditional Drenthe farm, but also how the younger generation of agriculturalists work with computers in their modern large-scale businesses.

Binnenpad

Some people call Giethoorn the Venice of the north. But that is an exaggeration, the similarity with the Italian city is that goods go by water.

Travelling through Giethoorn by punt is really an experience. The town was the location for the famous "Fanfare" film by Bert Haanstra, because he thought the scenery so attractive.

A punt is six metres long, one and half metres wide and only 15 centimetres deep.
The original long punting-pole is now replaced by an outboard motor.

Cutting reed

The village is eight kilometres long. More than one hundred bridges rise high above the village canal to allow punters to pass. The farmer used to take cows out to the pasture and fetch hay by punt, the shopkeeper delivered the groceries, the baker delivered bread, and the postman brought letters and newspapers, all by punt. This happens rarely nowadays, except for young couples who prefer to go to the Town Hall by boat on their wedding day. However, on the last Saturday evening in August, Giethoorn does look a little more like Venice. Then there is a "gondola tour" with decorated boats through a magically lit village.

Transport by punt

Harbour

Blokzijl was founded in the sixteenth century. Stadholder Jan van Ligne, Earl of Aremberg, commissioned the digging of a canal from Muggenbeet to the Zuider Zee with a lock, the "zijl", at the end. A small neighbourhood developed around the lock and it was fortified after the seige of Steenwijk (1580-81). Blokzijl with its protected inner harbour was of strategic importance and during the Eighty Years' War was a garrison town for Spanish troops. In 1672, the year of disaster, when the country was at war with France, Britain, Munster and Cologne, Stadholder William III granted town privileges because the inhabitants had brought the enemy to a halt.

The Reformed 17th century cruciform church was given an inbuilt tower in 1630 and later extended lengthways and across. The interior contains beautiful Renaissance furniture, baptismal railings, chandeliers and a fine model of a seventeenth century warship. Many beautiful houses on the Kerkstraat and Bierkade are the property of the Vereniging Hendrick de Keyser. Lovely seventeenth century patrician houses line the Bierkade, their elegant neck and step gables resemble the Amsterdam style of building. This is not surprising since there were close contacts with Holland.

Unfortunately the flowering of the newly made little town suddenly came to a halt at the end of the seventeenth century. The peat trade slumped because the hinterland became exhausted and the harbour silted up. Blokzijl lost its livelihood so quickly that one can hardly say it gradually fell into decline. The large harbour basin and the closely packed surrounding buildings fortunately remained, for the most part, in tact and therefore were saved.

Domine's wal

Bierkade

The IJsselmeer is easily reached from Blokzijl via the Vollenhovermeer and other lakes. And this together with the spacious harbour basin provides plenty of opportunity for lively and exciting water sports. This is currently an enormous source of wealth to Blokzijl.

Panorama of harbour

Lighthouse

Urk used to be an island and there is no place where people know more about the transformation of the Zuider Zee into the IJsselmeer.
The fishing industry had to be reorganised when the Afsluitdijk was closed in 1932.

Harbour

The government paid compensation according to tax returns. It was quite a problem because in hindsight few people were able to say that their tax returns were completely accurate, at least not in Urk.

However, the people of Urk continued to fish and fishing is still very important to them, even though they had to transfer activities to the ports of IJmuiden and Lauwersoog. Urk was permanently hooked onto the Noord-Oostpolder, yet it has still remained a village. New ideas might travel more easily over land, but they did not have much chance in Urk. The town remained loyal to its heritage, the fishing industry and the elegant costumes, and, of course, to the delightful singing of the Urk Male Voice Choir.

IJssel Bridge

Although Kampen behaved like a town long ago, the date when it received town privileges is unknown. Archaeological research points to a settlement in the eleventh century.

Many well conserved historical buildings in Kampen recall the long civic history of a once prosperous Hanseatic town. Kampen was an Imperial Free State City in 1495.

Cellebroederspoort

Koornmarktpoort

Broederpoort

The Koornmarktpoort (centre photo) from the fourteenth century is the only real defence gate in Kampen. Both towers were built on in the fifteenth century. The gateway was painted white in 1848.

At one time Kampen had 21 city gates. Only three have survived. As well as the Koornmarktpoort these are the Broederpoort (right, now the town museum) and the Cellebroederspoort (left, a student's club).

Vispoort

When wandering through Elburg you will be constantly surprised by the interesting views. After years of neglect many old buildings have now been restored and the numerous sights draw many tourists every year. It is not surprising that Elburg has been designated a protected townscape. Elburg was a thriving commercial centre in its heyday.
In the 16th and 17th centuries when commerce transferred more and more to the towns in Holland, Elburg's prosperity declined. Centuries later, the IJsselmeer impoldering provided new impulses through tourists attracted by the shore and yacht harbour.

The street plan of Elburg looks like a chess board and is considered to be one of the nicest examples of a medieval town layout. Parts of the medieval town wall, in particular on either side of the Vispoort, are still standing.
The Vispoort, a square wall tower dating from 1592 was once part of the town defences.
The Fishing Museum is housed on an upper floor. Some of the canon vaults, sixteenth century casemates, have withstood the wear and tear of time and been partly restored and opened to visitors.
You will not be bored in Elburg. The town has many interesting things to see, like the house

Vispoort

Town Museum

of Arent toe Boecop (1393) that was a town hall for centuries and is now the offices of the polder authority. There are also countless bell and step gables. The oldest residential house dates in part from the twelfth century. If you bypass Elburg, then you will miss a real treat.

Wall houses

Museum "de Waag"

On the Brink, in the mightiest Hanseatic town of the period, the Waag (weigh house) stands as a witness to Deventer's rich history.

The Waag, a museum nowadays, dates from 1528 and besides being a weigh house it was also the main guardhouse. It is a picturesque late gothic building with staircase tower and three small corner towers, and a wooden tower on the roof. A flight of renaissance steps was added in 1643 that harmonises well with the hundred year older building. A heavy kettle hangs on one of the walls where forgers were boiled alive in the mid-15th century. The Waag was seriously damaged by a bomb explosion in February 1945.

When approaching the city from the Veluwe, you will see the St Lebuinus church with the helmeted tower like a loyal soldier of the town standing on guard behind the impressive IJssel waterfront.

Panorama of River IJssel

Brink

The old centre is perhaps the most beautiful city centre in the Netherlands.

The Bergkwartier, east of the Brink, is a district with many historical buildings, nearly two hundred of these are listed monuments.

"De Bolwerksmolen", 1863

Bronkhorst is the smallest town in the Netherlands. A cheese factory is established in a 17th century farmhouse, Huize Ophemert or Het Hooghe Huys (The High House).
And actually the town is not much more than

several well preserved and restored houses and farmhouses grouped around the Chapel (1344). There are remains of the fourteenth century Bronkhorst Castle named after the gentlemen from Gelre who fought the Van Heeckerens. The castle was demolished in the last century. Slotheuvel is a nature reserve of 5 hectares where rare plants like the common dogwood, spindle tree, muskroot, and star of Bethlehem grow.

Panorama of the Rhine   *Sabelspoort*

The name Arneijm was recorded in 893. At the time it was not much more than a village, church and inn. It was given town privileges in 1233. The Sabelspoort is the only city gate which remains. In 1944 Arnhem was "a bridge too far" and the city and St Eusebius church were badly damaged in the battle. But it made plenty of space for a new city hall. Arnhem was rebuilt and the people sitting in the pavement cafes on the Korenmarkt hardly think about those difficult days.

Town Hall   *Korenmarkt*

De Waag

Nijmegen was not a bridge too far, but the city still suffered, in fact it was probably worse off, because the Allies bombed by mistake in February 1944.
The ancient town of the Roman and Carolingian empires suffered the worst year in its history.

Waal Bridge

Kronenburger Tower

But Nijmegen recovered and magnificently too. It is again a pleasure to walk along the Waal quay; St Stevens and the Town Hall have been restored, and the Waag (weigh house) on the Grote Markt is splendid.

In keeping with his high status, King-Stad-holder William III had to provide his country seat, Het Loo, with a costly and ingenious system to supply water to the high-spouting jets in the fountains of his French gardens. A complex network of pipes was constructed to transfer the water to the castle from high ground in the distance. The fountains in the forecourt operated on the principle of communicating vessels. The same method was applied to the pools in the forecourt, where horsemen once jostled to quench their thirst and water their horses.

(Top) Reception Hall
(Centre) Old dining room
(Bottom) Library

View of upper garden

Queen Beatrix officially opened the Rijksmuseum Paleis Het Loo in June 1984. The history of the House of Orange became visible where generations of Oranges had lived, from King-Stadholder William III to Queen Wilhelmina who died at the palace. Visitors can easily spend a whole day in the palace, garden and park, in what is called the Versailles of the North.

In the words of Queen Beatrix: the history of a house becomes the story of its occupants.

Bedroom of King Stadholder William III

Fishing boats in the harbour

The River Eem winds from Amersfoort to the north, to Spakenburg where they are famous for playing football, but never on Sundays. Where boatmen sail, anglers fish and professional fishermen do not give up easily. By the way, the fishing boats are marked with the BU of Bunschoten, a town which forms an entity with Spakenburg. The fishermen are properly dressed in traditional costume, entirely in black but with yellow clogs.

The men dress more simply than their women folk who take little notice of the latest fashion or gaping tourists. They remain faithful to the old costume, with the starched, flowery bodice that looks like the plastron of a medieval knight going to a tournament.

Town Hall

Statue of Comenius

Militiamen

On a stone tablet above the main entrance of the oldest town hall of the Gooi are the words "God is Almighty - AD 1601". A mere thirty years after the Spanish massacred the inhabitants and burnt the town down, the council could take up office in the new Town Hall. The present double moat was constructed after 1672 when the French captured the town. This unique monument of Dutch fortification has fortunately been preserved.

92 MUIDER CASTLE

Front view

(Top right) Bedroom
(Centre) P.C. Hooft Room

Muider Castle has guarded the mouth of the River Vecht since 1280. Floris V commissioned its building. He was the lord of the castle but also became a prisoner of rebellious lieges who murdered him near the castle in 1296.
The castle looked almost the same then as it does today. In 1609, Pieter Cornelisz Hooft became the castle governor and it was the beginning of an illustrious period. Plays were enacted, there was music and singing and lots of eating and drinking by the artistic and pleasure-seeking society that history calls the Muider Circle. The castle is a busily visited national museum.

Knights' Hall

Main entrance

Baron Van Zuylen van Nijevelt van de Haar had an impressive name and the castle De Haar is just as impressive. He had the castle built in 1892 by Cuypers, the architect of the Rijksmuseum and Central Station in Amsterdam. We might call his creation ''undutch''. It looks rather like a Bavarian fairy tale castle. A distant ancestor of the Baron, Dirk van Zuylen, mayor of Utrecht, an opponent of Duke Willem V, was left with a ruin after a visit in 1482 of the Duke's supporter, Egbert van Wassenaar. The castle was rebuilt half a century later. During the last rebuilding the whole hamlet of Haarzuilens was moved in order to landscape the garden around the castle.

The park is nearly always open to visitors, and there are conducted tours of the impressive castle.

Rose garden in winter

The 112 metres high Dom (cathedral) is the highest and most famous tower in the Netherlands and the most visited monument in the city. Every year, 75,000 people (including Philips II in 1549) puff their way up the 465 steps to enjoy the wonderful panorama 95 metres above the city bustle. This technical wonder acquired fame and glory for Utrecht because it is one of only five European church towers that exceed one hundred metres.

Dom tower

Oude Gracht

The former merchants' city does not have that many canals but they do give the centre a unique appearance. Outstanding features are the double arched bridges and very high quays. These were necessary to prevent flooding caused by high water levels. In 1374, the building of a lock in the Vaartsche Rijn near Vreeswijk meant that the canal water could be kept at the summer level.

Wharfs were built at the bottom of the quays so that ships could be unloaded there. The Oudegracht and Nieuwegracht (canals) therefore had two street levels, a rarity in Europe. Deep cellars were constructed under the street, opening onto the wharf to take in wine, merchandise, timber and especially turf. The wharfs and cellars are now ideal cafes, and the terraces on the wharfs are a colourful spectacle.

Standing back a little in a corner of Domplein is the Academy dating from 1894, the main seat of the university. In 1634
in the Groot-Kapittelhuis of the Dom, now the gothic showpiece of the university, the first lectures were held in theology, philosophy and law at the Illustre School. The faculty of medicine was founded in 1636.

University Academy
(Centre) Waag

Zoudebalch

On the Kromme Nieuwegracht is a sparkling building called Paus Huize and built in the Flemish style. The Leuven professor and cardinal Adriaen Florisz. Boeyens commissioned the building in 1517. He intended to live there, but his plan was foiled in 1522 when he was elected Pope. The only Dutch Pope died a year later. The Queen's Commissioner officially resides there now.

Paus Huize

Spherical houses

Oude Dieze

The Dutch song: "They're off to Den Bosch" means that there is going to be a lot of fun. Den Bosch is the short name for 's-Hertogenbosch. "Bossche bollen" are a Den Bosch delicacy, cakes shaped like balls and made of cream and chocolate. We could use the same name for the spherical houses pictured above.

The River Binnendieze winds through this lovely city.

In 1853, the city became a diocese once more, and the St Jan became a catholic cathedral again. The condition of the cathedral building was poor and generally people thought that the protestants had neglected the building. People are now more rational about this because the building work will never ever be completed.

St Jan's Cathedral

Genneper watermill

Eindhoven looks like a modern city without a past. However, this is definitely not true, since it is already 750 years old. But during the last hundred years, mainly thanks to the expansion of the Philips corporation, the city underwent a change of face.

Van Abbemuseum

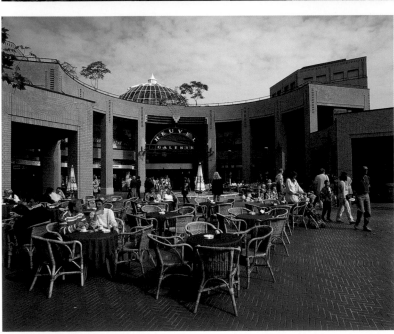

Heuvel Galerie

The Genneper is a very beautifully restored watermill that dates back well before 1249, when it was donated by deed to the Postel Abbey.
The seats on the Heuvel in the heart of the historic city look very convivial. However, the Evoluon opened in 1966 on the 75th anniversary of Philips is more representative of the city. The building looks like a flying saucer, 77 metres in diameter and 31 metres above ground.

Evoluon

Gouvernements Building

The Roman settlement Trajectum ad Mosam, the ford across the Maas, was established before AD 50, and at the end of the third century fortified like a castle.

It was mainly the bishop St Servatius who made the town important in the 4th century by transferring the bishop's seat from Tongeren to Maastricht.

The Servaas name is well-known in the city, both for the St Servaas church dating from 1000 (see opposite page) and for the St Servaas Bridge which dates from about 1300.

Jeker

Vrijthof

St Servaas Bridge

In 722 the bishop moved to Liège, but kept his privileges in the city.

The Onze Lieve Vrouwe Church (the bottom photo shows the rear of the church) remained his personal property. In 1632, Maastricht was captured by Frederik Hendrik.

St Jan's church, in the centre left photo pictured brotherly next to the St Servaas, has since belonged to the Reformed Church.

During the Belgian revolution in 1830, the city choose to side with the Netherlands. Since then it has been the capital of the Dutch province of Limburg.

The provincial authorities are called the "gouvernement" and have recently taken up office in a splendid bastion on the Maas.

St Servaas

The house on the Jeker

Maastricht is the most southern city in the Netherlands and has its own identity and character. On the Vrijthof, the large square behind the St Servaas, there are lots of pleasant pavement cafes and many a Dutch visitor from the north, could well imagine that here in the deep south, they were almost in a foreign country.

Onze Lieve Vrouwe Church

Thorn, the little white town, lies just inside the Netherlands. The old Abbey church has a bricked tower, but the rest of the interior is white.

The paving is decorated with geometric figures. But the nicest part is of course the whole impression which the white houses make.

These include stately patricians' houses, farm houses and simple village cottages of plastered brick. Some have monumental facades.

Through view

This town was a tiny independent state for eight hundred years.

In about 990, Hilsondis, countess of Strijen, together with her husband, count Ansfried van Hoei en Teisterbant, established a Benedictine convent. After Hilsondis' death, Ansfried became the bishop of Utrecht, but his daughter Hildewardis retained control over the Thorn convent founded by her parents.

And until 1794, noble ladies continued to reign as sovereign-abbesses with their own right to mint coins.

Wijlre   *(Top) Noorbeek*
                          (Right) Three-country-point

Zuid-Limburg is the most exotic area of the Netherlands. The half-timbered houses, as shown above, with brown beams and white faces, cannot be found anywhere else. Near Vijlen, the countryside becomes erotically rounded, something one would not expect in the Netherlands. In Vaals at the three-country-point, where the Dutch border meets those of Germany and Belgium, the 321 metre highest peak is a tourist attraction.

Cotessen

Statue of Michiel de Ruyter

Harbour

Museum Het Arsenaal

Michiel Adriaansz. de Ruyter was born in Vlissingen (Flushing) and his statue stands with his back to the arsenal on the boulevard which bears his name. The arsenal, a Napoleonic building, now contains the Maritime Attraction Centre.

Boulevard

The tower near the arsenal will give you a good long view of the ships on the Schelde. On the other side of the boulevard on the beach is the only remaining city tower, the Bomvrije.

Gevangen Tower

(Top right) "de Korenbloem"
Gable of the Manhuis

An impression of a quay in Goes surrounded by the lovely old facades of merchants' houses dating from the late Middle Ages.
Goes was once an important port. It still is an important place for water traffic, but nowadays it is mostly recreational.

Harbour

This has been one of the blessings of the Delta Works, particularly because of the creation of Lake Veere.

The Zeeland Bridge has made Goes more accessible by road and water to the many visitors from the Randstad (the western conurbation) who enjoy the pleasure boats in the harbour.

Manhuis garden

Haringvliet Bridge

Queen Juliana opened the Zeeland Bridge over the Eastern Schelde in 1965. It was not a part of the Delta Works but of such importance for access to Mid-Zeeland that the province itself had taken the initiative to build this.

The Eastern Schelde dam was put into operation by Queen Beatrix in October 1986 and the Delta Works were then officially complete.

The Delta Works were soon begun after the disastrous flooding of 1953. The storm flood barrier was operating in the Hollandse IJssel near Rotterdam in 1958. Noord-Beveland and Walcheren were connected by the Veerse Gat Dam in 1961.

The Volkerak Dam was under construction from 1957 to 1959 and the incorporated Hellegatsplein joined Hoekse Waard, Goeree-Overflakkee and Noord-Brabant together.

Zeeland Bridge

The Haringvliet Dam, between Voorne and Goeree, was completed in November 1970, and the Brouwers Dam, between Goeree and Schouwen, in May 1971. All the primary dams, except in the Eastern Schelde were then in operation.

There was a fierce political debate about an Eastern Schelde dam because of increasing concern about the environmental effects of a complete closure. The political compromise, a tidal dam is no mean feat from a technical point of view.

Sixty-six buttresses have been placed on the sea bed for a distance of 3,200 metres, each buttress is 45 metres high and weighs between 14,000 and 17,500 tons. Steel lift gates are hung between the concrete buttresses and can be let down as a protection against high tides.

Eastern Schelde Barrier

Storm Flood Barrier

Volkerak Locks

Town Hall

In the middle of the fifteenth century when English, Scottish, Italian, Spanish and Portuguese merchants had brought great prosperity to this city, a Town Hall was built. The city administrators wanted to show the world how important their town was. Flemish master builders of the Keldermans family built the beautiful late gothic Town Hall on the Markt, and after the church was demolished, the Town Hall could dominate the whole market square. However, when the Town Hall was completed trade had already past its peak.

The Norbertijner Abbey was founded in the 12th century.
Flemish monks built an abbey and chapel on a fortified hill which had already existed in the 9th century. Middelburg grew and flourished along with the abbey, and in 1217 gained town privileges, becoming the oldest town in Zeeland.
In its present restored state, the abbey dates from the 15th century, because it was almost completely gutted by fire in 1492.
After the Reformation it became the seat of the Provincial government. The Zeeuws Museum is also established there.

The Abbey

Battering ship "Schorpioen"

Kuiperspoort

Spijker Bridge

Middelburg, the pearl in the heart of Walcheren, is the capital of Zeeland. The province with the motto: "Luctor et emergo, I struggle and emerge". The heraldic Zeeland lion struggles and emerges out of the water. The foreign merchants of old may have disappeared from the capital, but there are now more and more foreign tourists. Hardly a surprise because it is a town which you must see and experience for yourself. On Thursdays for instance on the Markt, when the whole of the population of Walcheren seems to be in town.

St Jorisdoelen

Town Hall

The gothic Town Hall, dating from 1474, designed by the Antwerp architect Spoorwater, reveals the glory of a rich history. The tower, from 1599, can be seen for miles around.
The little corbelled towers on the corners are a delight.
On top of the tower is a wind vane consisting of a ship with five flags, three of Van Borssele, one of the House of Orange and one of Zeeland.

Harbour

Campveerse Tower

The Campveerse Tower (1500) on the quay wall still guards the mouth of the harbour.
In 1551, Veere received stowing rights for Scottish wool and the wool trade flourished. The Scottish colony enjoyed special privileges and the Scottish houses on the quay are still proof of this. But the glorious days of Veere eventually faded. The Great Church was turned into a hospital, stables and barracks. It has now been restored and is used for exhibitions.
After an era of great decline, the town is thriving again. The merchant ships have been replaced by pleasure craft because Lake Veere has brought new prosperity.

Windmill "de Koe" 1909

St Lievensmonster Church

Zierikzee is a lively Zeeland monument. The most outstanding feature of the Town Hall, constructed at the end of the fourteenth century, is the sturdy tower which is crowned by a gracious spire. The spire sports a golden plated Neptune which emphasises the link with the sea.

Stadhuis

Zuidhavenpoort

The St Lievenmonster Tower demonstrates that the once sky-high ambitions of the town were later limited.
The varying years of wealth, poverty, growth and decline are definitely over.
The Delta Works brought new life into the town. Large gates like the Zuidhavenpoort and the Noordhavenpoort and many other beautiful monuments make the town into one big museum.

Oude Haven N.Z.

Noordhavenpoort

Harbour

The fame of Yerseke, oyster cultivation, dates from the end of the last century. Because it first seemed likely that this industry would be lost when the Eastern Schelde was closed from the sea, alternative locations had to be sought. This was an unfortunate, but necessary measure.

Oyster tanks

However, the half-open tidal dam in the Eastern Schelde was able to turn the tide, and plans were changed.

Then nobody could anticipate that severe winters and an unexpected disease would be another serious threat to the oysters.
But Yerseke is still there and oyster cultivation has continued.

Harbour

Vegetable Garden of Europe

The density of greenhouses gives the Westland its nickname 'Glass City'.
It is the vegetable garden of Western Europe, although flower cultivation is also very important.
Naaldwijk is the centre of this area, and the local Westland museum is situated there.

Hidden among the greenhouses of the Westland are a number of villages: Maasland, De Lier, Schipluiden, Wateringen and Monster, each of which are historical sights in their own right.
's-Gravenzande is not a village but a real town.

Euromast

Rotterdam gained town privileges in 1340, but apart from St Laurens Church and the Schielandshuis there are few old historical monuments. The reason is the bombardment of Rotterdam on 14 May 1940, when the whole historical centre went up in flames.

Beside the Maas tunnel, which was almost secretly opened in 1942, the Euromast was built in 1960 for the Floriade horticultural exhibition.

Delfshaven

A Space Tower was placed on top in 1970. The Euromast has now been taken over in height by the building of the Nationale Nederlanden on the Weena.

In 1886 Delfshaven became a part of Rotterdam. It is now a wonderfully preserved historical district, with an historical ambience which Rotterdam itself had lost.

Delfshaven

Willem Bridge panorama

Where the new Willem bridge greets the city, was once the site when the River Rotte originally flowed into a bend of the River Maas. The bend was washed by the ebb and flow of the river, and it became the harbour mouth. The New Waterway was finished in 1871, after which the development of docks began, via Zuid, Pernis, Botlek and Europoort, on to the Maasvlakte.

Europoort

Container terminal

In 1963 Rotterdam could call itself "the biggest port in the world", i.e. the port handling the largest quantity of cargo. This has remained a proud, unbroken record to this day.

A greater difference is hardly imaginable.
On one side of the River Noord, the twentieth
century docks and industrial area of Rijnmond
and on the other the rural activities of the
Alblasserwaard.
And on the border are the windmills of
Kinderdijk, a complete series of no less than
nineteen windmills. It is hardly a wonder that
half the world (at least in tourist terms) has to
see this!

Nineteen windmills in all, of which seventeen are in operation en mass on Saturday afternoons in July and August.
The inside of a mill can then also be viewed. The mills remove surplus water from the polders to the surrounding storage water. On the right are the top-wheelers, hexagonal windmills with a thatched roof. The mills on the left are also top-wheelers, but they are round and built entirely of brick.

Is it true that during the St Elisabeth flooding of 1421, a baby floated past in a cradle, accompanied by a cat to keep the cradle from toppling?

The story is too nice, but Kinderdijk owes its name to this legend. There is a house on the Oost Kinderdijk that has a wall plaque commemorating it.

Gouda was a prominent town in Holland which received town privileges in 1272.

The building of the late gothic Town Hall of Gouda was begun in 1448. The main entrance was embellished with a fine flight of Renaissance steps designed by the Gouda sculptor, Gregorius Cool, in 1603.

The front facade was extensively restored at the end of the last century, and another overall restoration took place in the early 1950s.

Toll House

De Waag

Binnenhavenmuseum, Turfsingel   *"de Roode Leeuw" 1680 (top)*

In foreign countries, Gouda cheese is often synonymous with Dutch cheese.

Cheese used to be weighed in the Waag, a building dating from 1688 and designed by Pieter Post.

The relief in the gable, depicting the weighing of cheese, does not leave anyone in doubt as to the purpose of the building.

The importance of the cheese market has even increased in our times because of the concentration of markets.

Town Hall

After a serious fire, only the square tower with its sturdy brick base remained of the original medieval Town Hall in Delft. It dates from the 13th century, the stone upper structure was erected at the end of the 15th century.
This tower is surrounded on three sides by a building designed by Hendrick de Keyser and constructed between 1618 and 1620.

Old Church

Town Hall

Vleeshal

In the 17th century grave monuments were erected to Tromp and Piet Hein in the Old Church. Delft together with Delfshaven was an important maritime town.
The Vleeshal (see above) was a meat hall and dates from about 1660. On the Koornmarkt the buildings continue along into the canal.
The Dutch Military and Weapons Museum is accommodated in the former arsenal of the Staten van Holland.

Armamentarium

Delft is mainly famous as the Orange Town. The Great Church, of which the tower is visible in the background of this photograph, contains the family vaults of the House of Orange. These are not open to the public. But the tomb of William of Orange can be viewed in the church.

The work on the mausoleum of white and black marble, designed by Hendrick de Keyser, took eight years to finish. At William's feet lies the dog that is said to have stopped eating when its master died and which quickly followed him into eternity.

This all happened nearby, in the Prinsenhof. In conclusion, probably the most photographed site in Delft, the Vrouwenregt. The little bridge over the canal leads to the Kerkstraat, with the high wall of the church rising up on one side.

Langendijk

Oostpoort

Vrouwenregt

Binnenhof, Parliament building

Lower House

Hofvijver

The Binnenhof is the beating heart of Dutch parliamentary democracy. All the occupants of the past have contributed something of their own to the buildings which make the Binnenhof what it is today: a picture book of national history. The photograph next to the Binnenhof shows the chamber of the Lower House.

In the wintery scene, there are skaters on the Hofvijver. In the centre is the Mauritshuis Museum and directly to the left, the famous little tower which is the office of the Dutch Prime Minister.

Noordeinde Palace

Opening of parliament   *Binnenhof*

Noordeinde Palace is the office of Queen
Beatrix and only a stone's throw from the
Binnenhof and parliament. The palace dating
from 1533 was furnished in 1590 for Louise de
Coligny, the widow of William of Orange.
The residential palace of the Queen is Huis ten
Bosch. On the third Tuesday in September,
parliament is opened by the Queen, a special
occasion when she arrives in the Golden
Coach. It is an important event in the Dutch
calendar.

Mauritshuis

Plein 1813

Lighthouse

Scheveningen has always belonged to The Hague, and yet remains a separate community which upholds its own traditions such as costume.

The town council gave the fishing fleet its own harbour in 1904, which soon became too small. Fishing and the fish auction are still important to Scheveningen. But since it opened in 1972, the yacht harbour has grown considerably. There is also a ferry service from Scheveningen to the English port of Great Yarmouth.

Kurhaus

When the council of The Hague agreed in 1973 to the proposals for a new development of the seaside resort, a great many changes were to take place. Not everyone was happy about these changes, but thanks to the efforts of the Countess of Limburg Stirum and her company for the preservation of the Kurhaus and Scheveningen and also thanks to the citizens of The Hague, Scheveningen and the Kurhaus were saved from the proposed demolition. Extensive renovation restored the Kurhaus to its former glory.

In 1868, Scheveningen was already an important resort with public baths, two large hotels and the first horse-driven tram in the Netherlands that ran from the Kneuterdijk in The Hague. There was at that time already a request for a concession for a pier, but it was 1901 before the pier was opened. It was called after Queen Wilhelmina, an idea of Prince Hendrik, the Queen's husband who conducted the opening ceremony. The pier was an immediate success, and stood until the spring of 1942.

Pier

Scheveningen was evacuated in 1942 when the Atlantic Wall was under construction. A year later the pier was in ruins, it was demolished after a fire. A useless act because the Pier was completely unsuitable for landing troops or other military activities. Scheveningen had to wait until 1961 before the next Prince of the Netherlands, Bernhard, came to open the next Pier.

Traditional costume

Beach

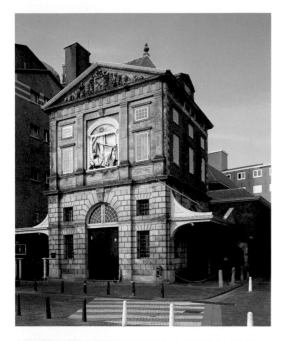
De Waag

Leiden is a town of many faces, but in the first place it is and has remained a university town, since 1575.

It is the oldest university town in the Netherlands, founded by William of Orange in appreciation of the population's courageous resistance during the siege of Leiden in 1574. The population could choose between a university or taxation benefits. So the decision was a university. You cannot actually miss the university because it is established in both the old city centre as well as the suburbs.

The Academy Building on the Rapenburg houses the Senates Chamber and the Great Auditorium.

Morschpoort

Hartebrug Church

Koorn Bridge

Academy on the Rapenburg

Stevenshofje

But there is much more to see. A random selection: the Waag (weigh house), Morschpoort and Koorn Bridge and behind the latter, the Town Hall. And finally the Hartebrug Church of 1835.

Eva van Hoogeveen hofje

There is not a town in the Netherlands with more "hofjes" courtyards than Leiden.
It has about 35 in all, and a great many are worth a visit.
The VVV Tourist Office has a special leaflet on courtyards, which lists the most important for a walking tour. The largest courtyard is Meermansburg established at the end of 17th century. The Pijpenkabinet, a museum for clay tobacco pipes is situated there.

Hof Meermansburg   *Pietershof*

St Jacobshofje

The Flora flower auction and the Rijnsburg flower parade are well-known in Holland. But this region is even more famous as the bulb growing area.
The Keukenhof garden in Lisse is the ideal place to go to enjoy splendid flowers. You will be reminded of the first bulbs which were grown by Clusius in the Hortus Botanicus in Leiden not many miles from here.

Flower parade (far right)